contents

MW00609030

cozy mitten scarf

Yarn (5)

Lion Brand® *Jiffy*, 3oz/85g skeins, each approx 135yd/123m (acrylic)
- 4 skeins in Country Green #181 (A)
- 2 skeins in Apple Green #132 (B)

Hooks
- Size M/13 (9.00mm) crochet hook
- Size K/10½ (6.50mm) crochet hook
or size needed to obtain gauge

Notions
- Tapestry needle
- Straight or safety pins

Finished Measurements
92"/233.5cm by 10.5"/26.5cm including edging

Gauges
- 9 sts and 7 rows to 4"/10cm over pattern st for scarf.
- 12 sts and 10 rows to 4"/10cm over pattern st for mittens.
Take time to check gauges.

Note
Ch-2 counts as 1 hdc

Stitch Glossary
Loop St Worked with WS facing, insert hook in next st, pass yarn around your index finger held 1"–1½"/ 2.5–4cm away from the work, yo, making sure to catch working yarn on the side closest to your skein, pull through st, yo, pull through 2 loops on hook.

Scarf
With A and larger hook, ch 23.
Row 1 Sc in 2nd ch from hook, dc in next ch, *sc in next ch, dc in next ch, repeat from * across. Ch 1, turn—11 sc +11 dc.
Row 2 Sc in 1st dc, dc in next sc, *sc in next dc, dc in next sc. Rep from * across. Ch 1, turn. Repeat Row 2 for pattern until work measures 92"/233.5cm from start. End off.

Mittens (make 2)
With B and smaller hook, ch 21.
Row 1 Sc in 2nd ch from hook and in each ch across. Ch 2, turn—20 sc.
Row 2 Hdc in each sc across to last sc, 2 hdc in last sc. Ch 1, turn—21 hdc.
Row 3 2 Sc in each hdc across. Ch 2, turn—22 sc.
Row 4 Rep Row 2—23 hdc.
Row 5 Rep Row 3—24 sc.
Rows 6–8 Work even in pattern as established, 1 row hdc, 1 row sc, 1 row hdc.
Row 9 Sc2tog, sc in each hdc to end. Ch 2, turn—23 sc.
Row 10 Hdc in each sc across to last 2 sc, hdc2tog. Ch1, turn—22 hdc.
Rows 11 & 12 Rep Rows 9–10.
Row 13 Sc2tog, sc in each of next 7 hdc, ch 8, sc in 2nd ch from hook and in each of next 7 ch, ch 3, turn, hdc in each sc to end of thumb,

ch 1, turn, sc in each dc across, sk 2 hdc of Row 12, sc in next hdc of Row 12 and in each hdc to end.

First Mitten
Ch 1, rotate ¼ turn clockwise to work across cuff.

Second Mitten
End off. Turn work, join yarn at opposite side of cuff with sl st, ch 1.

Cuff
Row 1 (RS) Work 12 sc evenly spaced across cuff edge. Ch 1 turn.
Row 2 (WS) Loop st in each sc across. Ch 1, turn.
Row 3 Sc in each loop st across. Ch 1, turn.
Rows 4–5 Rep Rows 2 & 3. End off.

Mitten Finishing
With B and smaller hook, work 1 row sc evenly spaced across top/curved edge of mitten. Tack down base of thumb to skipped hdcs.

Finishing
Edging
With B and larger hook, work 1 rnd sc evenly spaced around entire scarf, placing 3 sc in each corner. End off.
Pin Mittens into place approx 2"/5cm up from short edge of scarf, making sure thumbs point inwards.
With B and a tapestry needle, sew Mittens into place.
Weave in all ends.■

reader's wrap

Yarn 4
Bernat® Sheep(ish) by Vickie Howell, 3oz/85g skeins, each approx 167yd/153m (acrylic/wool)
• 5 skeins in Pink(ish) #0008

Hook
• Size I/9 (5.50 mm) crochet hook *or size needed to obtain gauge*

Notions
• Tapestry needle
• Straight or safety pins

Finished Measurements
Across back 27"/69cm
Length from inside neck 16"/41cm

Gauge
24 sts/6 reps and 12 rows to 4"/10cm over pattern stitch.
Take time to check gauge

Stitch Glossary
Shell (sc, ch 2, sc) in specified stitch.

Scarf
Back
Ch 62.
Row 1 Shell in 2nd ch from hook, *sk 2 ch, shell in next ch. Rep from * to end. Ch 1, turn—21 shells.
Row 2 Shell in 1st sc, shell in 1st ch-2 sp, *shell in next ch-2 sp. Rep from * across, shell in last sc. Ch 1, turn—23 shells.
Rows 3 and 4 Shell in 1st ch-2 sp and in each ch-2 sp across. Ch 1, turn—23 shells.
Rep Rows 2–4 for pattern until row has 43 shells in it, ending with a Row 4. Should measure approx 11"/28cm from start.

Right Scarf Front
Row 1 Shell in 1st ch-2 sp and in each of next 14 ch-2 sps. Ch 1, turn—15 shells.
Row 2 Shell in 1st ch-2 sp and in each ch-2 sp across. Ch 1, turn.
Rep Row 2 for pattern until work measures 16"/40.5cm from start of Front. End off.

Left Scarf Front
Row 1 Sk 13 shells in center of last row of Back, shell in next ch-2 sp and in each ch-2 sp across. Ch 1, turn—15 shells.
Row 2 Shell in 1st ch-2 sp and in each ch-2 sp across. Ch 1, turn.
Rep Row 2 for pattern until work measures 16"/40.5cm from start of Front. End off.

Large Pocket (make 1)
Ch 35.
Row 1 Shell in 2nd ch from hook, *sk 2 ch, shell in next ch. Rep from * to end. Ch 1, turn—11 shells.
Row 2 Shell in 1st ch-2 sp and in each ch-2 sp across. Ch 1, turn.
Rep Row 2 for pattern until work measures 6"/15cm. End off.

Small Pockets (make 2)
Ch 14.
Rep all instructions for Large Pocket—5 shells.

Finishing
Edgings
Edge bottom of Back by working 1 row of shells in opposite side of foundation ch, with each edging shell in the same ch as each original shell. End off.
Edge the bottom of all three pockets in the same manner as Back Edging.
Pin pockets into place at 1"/2.5cm from bottom edge and sides of scarf, with Large pocket on Right Front and 2 Small Pockets on Left Front. Sew into place leaving top edge open.
Weave in all ends. ■

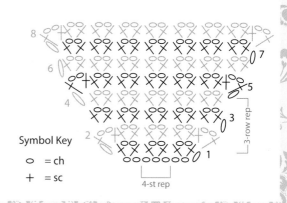

Symbol Key
o = ch
+ = sc

4-st rep
3-row rep

child's owl scarves

Yarn ④

RED HEART *Soft Baby Steps Solids*, 5oz/141g skeins, each approx 256yd/234m (acrylic)
- 2 skeins in Baby Blue #9800 OR Baby Pink #9700 (A)

RED HEART *Soft Baby Steps Prints*, 4oz/113g skeins, each approx 204yd/187m (acrylic)
- 1 skein Blue Earth Print #9935 OR Cherry Cola Print #9934 (B)

RED HEART *Soft*, 5oz/141g skeins, each approx 256yd/234m (acrylic)
- 1 skein Toast #1882 (C)
- Small amounts worsted weight yarn in white, black and orange.

Hook
- Size H/8 (5mm) crochet hook *or size needed to obtain gauge*

Notions
- Tapestry needle
- Straight or safety pins
- Stitch marker

Finished Measurements
44"/112cm by 5"/13cm

Gauge
16 sts and 12 rows to 4"/10cm over sc.
Take time to check gauge.

Note
Ch-2 counts as hdc throughout.

Scarf
With A, ch 22.
Row 1 Sc in 2nd ch from hook and in each ch across. Ch 2, turn—21 sc.
Row 2 Sk 1st sc, 2 hdc in next sc. *sk 1 sc, 2 hdc in next sc. Rep from * to across, hdc in last sc. Ch 1, turn—10 2-hdc shells + 2 hdc.
Row 3 Sc in each hdc across. Ch 2, turn.
Rep Rows 2–3 until scarf measures 44"/112cm or desired length, ending with a Row 3. End off.

Owl (make 2)
Rnds are worked in a spiral, mark 1st st of each rnd to keep track.
With B, ch 2.
Rnd 1 6 sc in 2nd ch from hook.
Rnd 2 2 sc in each sc around—12 sc.
Rnd 3 (2 sc in next sc, sc in next sc) 6 times—18 sc.
Rnd 4 (2 sc in next sc, sc in each of next 2 sc) 6 times—24 sc.
Rnd 5 (2 sc in next sc, sc in each of next 3 sc) 6 times—30 sc.
Rnd 6 (2 sc in next sc, sc in each of next 4 sc) 6 times. End off—36 sc.
Rnd 7 Change to C, sl st in 1st sc of rnd, ch 3, dc in same sc as sl st, dc in each of next 2 sc, (2 dc in next sc, dc in each of next 2 sc) 11 times. Join rnd with sl st in top of beg-ch. Ch 3, do not turn—48 dc.
Remainder of Owl is worked in rows.
Row 1 Dc in same st as sl st, dc in each of next 8 dc, 2 dc in next dc. Ch 3, turn—12 dc.
Row 2 Dc in 1st dc, dc in each of next 10 dc, 2 dc in last dc. Ch 3, turn—14 dc.
Row 3 Dc2tog, dc in each of next 8 dc, dc2tog, dc. Ch 3, turn—12 dc.
Row 4 Dc2tog, dc in each of next 6 dc, dc2tog. Ch 3, turn—10 dc.
Row 5 Dc2tog, ch 3, sl st in each of next 4 dc, ch 3, dc2tog, dc in last dc. End off.

Eyes (make 2)
With white scrap yarn, ch 2.
Rnd 1 6 sc in 2nd ch from hook.
Rnd 2 2 sc in each sc around.
Rnd 3 (2 sc in 1st sc, sc in next sc) 6 times. Join rnd with sl st in 1st sc. End off.

Finishing
Sew eyes onto each owl as shown in photo.
With black, embroider 3 French knots in each eyeball for pupils.
With orange, embroider a beak on each owl.
Pin owls into place on each scarf end.
Stitch into place with C, working all the way around body but just tacking the sides of the head.
Weave in all ends. ■

granny square scarf

Yarn 🔢2

Premier Yarns Deborah Norville Collection *Serenity Garden Yarn*, 2¼ oz/65g skeins, each approx 185yd/169m (micro fiber)
• 4 skeins in Hibiscus #0003 (A)
Premier Yarns Deborah Norville Collection *Serenity Sock Solids Yarn*, 1¾oz/50g skeins, each approx 230yd/210m (merino/nylon/rayon)
• 1 skein in Red #5003 (B)

Hooks
• Size G/6 (4.00mm) crochet hook
• Size F/5 (3.75mm) crochet hook
or size needed to obtain gauge

Notions
• Tapestry needle
• 2¾"/2cm buttons

Finished Measurements
64"/163cm by 8"/20cm

Gauge
20 sts and 4 rounds to 4"/10cm over motif stitch pattern.
Take time to check gauge.

Note
Granny squares are joined as you go.
Ch-3 counts as 1 dc.
Ch-5 counts as dc + ch-2.
Ch-6 counts as 1 dc + ch-3.

Stitch Glossary
Corner (3 dc, ch 2, 3 dc) in designated st.

First Granny Square
Ch 4, join into ring with sl st in 1st ch.
Rnd 1 Ch 5, 3 dc in ring, *ch 2, 3 dc in ring. Rep from * twice more, ch 2, 2 dc in ring. Join rnd with sl st in 3rd ch of beg-ch-5—4 3-dc shells.
Rnd 2 Sl st in 1st ch-2 sp, ch 5, 3 dc in same ch-2 sp, *ch 1, corner in next ch-2 sp; Rep from * twice more, ch 1, 2 dc in 1st ch-2 sp. Join rnd with sl st in 3rd ch of beg-ch-5.
Rnd 3 Sl st in 1st ch-2 sp, ch 5, 3 dc in same ch-2 sp, *ch 1, 3 dc in next ch-1 sp, ch 1, corner in next ch-2 sp; rep from * twice more, ch 1, 3 dc in next ch-1 sp, ch 1, 2 dc in 1st ch-2 sp. Join rnd with sl st in 3rd ch of beg-ch-5.
Rnd 4 Sl st in 1st ch-2 sp, ch 5, 3 dc in same ch-2 sp, *(ch 1, 3 dc in next ch-1 sp) twice, ch 1, corner in next ch-2 sp; rep from * twice more, (ch 1, 3 dc in next ch-1 sp) 2 times, ch 1, 2 dc in 1st ch-2 sp. Join rnd with sl st in 3rd ch of beg-ch-5.
Rnds 5–8 Work in pattern as established, placing corner in each corner and 3 dc in each ch-1 sp on each side, with a ch-1 before and after each. There will be one more ch-1 sp/3-dc shell on each side after every rnd. End off after Rnd 8.

Additional Granny Squares (make 7)
Rnds 1–7 Rep Rnds 1–7 of First Granny Square
Rnd 8 Sl st in 1st ch-2 sp, ch 5, 3 dc in same ch-2 sp, (ch 1, 3 dc in next ch-1 sp) 6 times, ch 1, corner in next ch-2 sp, (ch 1, 3 dc in next ch-1 sp) 6 times, ch 1, 3 dc in corner ch-2 sp, ch 1, sl st in corresponding corner of previous Granny Square, 3 dc in corner ch-2 sp, *sl st in corresponding ch-1 sp of previous granny square, 3 dc in next ch-1 sp; rep from *5 times more, ch 1, 3 dc in corner ch-2 sp, ch 1, sl st in corresponding ch-2 sp of previous granny square, 3 dc in corner ch-2 sp, **ch 1, 3 dc in next ch-1 sp; rep from ** 5 times more, ch 1, 2 dc in 1st ch-2 sp. Join rnd with sl st in 3rd ch of beg-ch-5. End off.

Pockets (make 2)
Rnds 1–7 Rep Rnds 1–7 of First Granny Square.
Rnd 8 Place pocket on top of Granny Square at end of scarf. Sl st in 1st ch-2 sp, ch 4, sl st in corresponding ch-2 sp of Granny Square on Scarf, ch 1, 3 dc in next ch-1 sp. Work in same manner as Rnd 8 of Additional Granny Square, joining the Pocket to the Scarf on three sides, then finishing the Rnd across top of Pocket. End off.

Flower 1 (make 4)
With smaller hook and B, ch 5, join into ring with sl st in 1st ch.
Rnd 1 12 sc in ring. Join rnd with sl st in 1st sc.
Rnd 2 Ch 6, sk next sc, dc in next sc, (ch 3, sk 1 sc, dc in next sc) 4 times, ch 3, join rnd with sl st in 3rd ch of beg-ch-6—6 ch-3 sps
Rnd 3 Sl st in 1st ch-3 sp, ch 3, 3 dc in same ch-3 sp, (ch 4, 4 dc in next ch-3 sp) 5 times, ch 4, join rnd with sl st in top of beg-ch.
Rnd 4 Sl st in next dc, ch 1, sc between dc with sl st just made and next dc, ch 2, [dc in next ch-4 sp, (ch 1, dc in same ch-4 sp) twice, ch 3, dc in same ch-4 sp, (ch 1, dc in same ch-4 sp) twice, ch 2, sc between 2nd and 3rd dc from hook] 6 times, replacing last sc with sl st in 1st sc to join rnd. End off.

Flower 2 (make 2)
With smaller hook and B, ch 5, join into ring with sl st in 1st ch.
Rnd 1 Ch 5, dc in ring, (ch 2, dc in ring) 4 times, ch 2, join rnd with sl st in 3rd ch of beg-ch—8 ch-2 sps
Rnd 2 Ch 6, dc in next dc, (ch 3, dc in next dc) 6 times, ch 3, join rnd with sl st in 3rd ch of beg-ch.

Rnd 3 Ch 1, sc in same st as join, (ch 4, sc in next dc) 7 times, ch 4, join rnd with sl st in 1st sc.

Rnd 4 Ch 1, sc in same st as join, (sc, 5 dc, sc in next ch-4 sp, sc in next sc) 8 times, replacing last sc with sl st in 1st sc to join rnd. End off.

Finishing

Sew buttons to scarf; ch-1 sp on pocket serves as buttonhole. Sew 3 flowers across top of each pocket using photo as guide.

Weave in all ends. ∎

cabled pocket scarf

Yarn (5)

Bernat® Alpaca™ *Natural Blends*, 3½oz/100g skeins, each approx 120yd/110m (acrylic/alpaca)

• 11 skeins in Peony #93420

Hook

• Size J/10 (6.00mm) crochet hook *or size needed to obtain gauge*

Notions

• Tapestry needle
• Straight or safety pins

Finished Measurements

100"/254cm by 12"/30.5cm excluding fringe

Gauges

• 12 sts and 5 rows to 4"/10cm over stitch pattern for scarf.
• 11 sts and 6 rows to 4"/10cm over stitch pattern for pocket.

Take time to check gauges.

Note

Ch 3 counts as 1 dc throughout.

Stitch Glossary

Fptr On RS row, work a treble crochet around the post of designated st instead of through its loops (see diagram for exact placement). Yo hook twice, insert hook around post, yo, draw through st, (yo, draw through two loops on hook) 3 times.

Bptr On WS row, work as for fptr around the RS of fptr.

Scarf

Ch 38.

Row 1 Dc in 4th ch from hook and in each ch across. Ch 3, turn—35 dc.

Row 2 (RS) Dc in next dc, *fptr in next dc, dc in next dc. Rep from * to last dc, dc in last dc. Ch 3, turn.

Row 3 (WS) Dc in next dc, *bptr in next fptr, dc in next dc. Rep from * to last dc, dc in last dc. Ch 3, turn.

Row 4 Dc in next dc, *fptr in next bptr, dc in next dc; rep from * to last dc, dc in last dc. Ch 3, turn.

Row 5 Rep Row 3.

Rep Rows 4–5 for pattern until scarf measures 100"/254cm or desired length, ending with a Row 5. Ch 1, turn.

Scarf Edging

Rnd 1 Work 1 rnd sc evenly spaced around entire scarf, placing 3 sc in each corner. End off.

Pocket (make 2)

Ch 30.

Row 1 Dc in 4th ch from hook and in each ch across. Ch 3, turn—28 dc.

Row 2 (RS) Dc in each of next 2 dc, (fptr in same dc as last dc worked, fptr in next dc, sk 2 dc, fptr in next 2 dc, dc in same dc as last fptr worked, dc in next 4 dc) twice, fptr in same dc as last dc worked, fptr in next dc, sk 2 dc, fptr in next 2 dc, dc in same dc as last fptr worked, dc in last 2 dc. Ch 3, turn—12 fptr, 16 dc.

Row 3 (WS) Dc in each of next 2 dc, (sk 1st 2 fptr, bptr around next 2 fptr, working in front of sts just made, bptr around skipped 2 fptr, dc in next 5 dc) twice, sk 2 fptr, bptr around next 2 fptr, working in front of sts just made, bptr around skipped 2 fptr, dc in last 3 dc. Ch 3, turn.

Row 4 Dc in next dc, (sk next dc, fptr around next 2 bptr, dc in same bptr as fptr just made, dc in next bptr, fptr around next 2 bptr, sk next dc, dc in next 3 dc) twice, sk next dc, fptr around next 2 bptr, dc in same bptr as fptr just made, dc in next bptr, fptr around next 2 bptr, sk next dc, dc in last 2 dc. Ch3, turn.

Row 5 Dc in next dc, (bptr around next 2 fptr, dc in next 2 dc, bptr around next 2 fptr, dc in next 3 dc) twice, bptr around next 2 fptr, dc in next 2 dc, bptr around next 2 fptr, dc in last 3 dc. Ch 3, turn.

Row 6 Dc in next dc, (fptr around next 2 bptr, dc in next 2 dc, fptr around next 2 bptr, dc in next 3 dc) rep twice, fptr around next 2 bptr, dc in next 2 dc, fptr around next 2 bptr, dc in the last 2 dc. Ch 3, turn.

Row 7 Dc in the next dc, dc in the 1st fptr, (bptr in each of the next 4 fptr, skipping middle 2 dc, dc in last fptr, dc in next 3 dc, dc in next fptr) twice, bptr in each of the next 4 fptr, skipping middle 2 dc, dc in last fptr, dc in last 2 dc. Ch 3, turn.

Row 8 Dc in next 2 dc, (sk 1st 2 bptr, fptr around next 2 bptr, working in front of sts just made, fptr around skipped 2 bptr, dc in next 5 dc) twice, sk 2 bptr, fptr around next 2 bptr, working in front of sts just made, fptr around skipped 2 bptr, dc in last 3 dc. Ch 3, turn.

Row 9 Dc in next dc, (sk next dc, bptr around next 2 fptr, dc in same fptr as bptr just made, dc in next fptr, bptr around fptr just worked, bptr in next fptr, sk next dc, dc in next 3 dc) twice, sk next dc, bptr around next 2 fptr, dc in same fptr as bptr just made, dc in next fptr, bptr around fptr just worked, bptr in next fptr, sk next dc, dc in last 2 dc. Ch 3, turn.

Row 10 Dc in next dc, (fptr around next 2 bptr, dc in next 2 dc, fptr around next 2 bptr, dc in next 3 dc) twice, fptr around next 2 bptr, dc in next 2 dc, fptr around next 2 bptr, dc in last 2 dc. Ch 3, turn.

Row 11 Rep Row 5.

Row 12 Dc in the next dc, dc in the 1st bptr, (fptr in each of the next 4 bptr, skipping middle 2 dc, dc in last bptr, dc in next 3 dc, dc in next bptr) twice, fptr in each of the next 4 bptr, skipping middle 2 dc, dc in last bptr, dc in last 2 dc. Ch 3, turn.

Row 13 Rep Row 3.

Row 14 Rep Row 4.

Row 15 Rep Row 5. End off.

Pocket Edging

Rnd 1 Join with sl st in any st of pocket, ch 1, sc around, join rnd with sl st to 1st sc.

Finishing

Cut 140 22"/56cm lengths of yarn for fringe. Thread 2 strands evenly through each sc at short ends of scarf. Gather fringe in groups of 10 and overhand knot at approx 1"/2.5cm from scarf edge.

Center Pockets on RS of scarf 5"/13cm from edge, and pin into place. Sew together with tapestry needle, leaving the top edge open.

Weave in all ends. ■

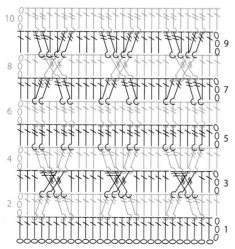

Symbol Key

0 = ch

= dc

= fptr

= bptr

double pocket scarf

Yarn 6 5

Premier Yarns Deborah Norville Collection *Cuddle Fleece*, 3½oz/100g skeins, each approx 110yd/100m (polyester)
• 5 skeins in Circus #5001 (A)
Premier Yarns Deborah Norville Collection *Serenity Chunky Solids*, 3½oz/100g skeins, each approx 109yd/100m (acrylic)
• 1 skein in Molten Lava #7033 (B)

Hooks
• Size P/15 (11.5mm) crochet hook
• Size N/13 (9.00 mm) crochet hook
• Size L/11 (8.00 mm) crochet hook
or size needed to obtain gauge

Notions
• Tapestry needle
• Straight or safety pins

Finished Measurements
61"/155 m by 7"/18cm including edging

Gauges
• 10 sts and 8 rows to 4"/10cm over scblo with A and larger hook.
• 8.5 sts and 5 rows to 4"/10cm over dc with B and smaller hook.
Take time to check gauges.

Stitch Glossary
Scblo (single crochet in back loop only) Work a single crochet in the back loop of the stitch.

Note
Ch-3 counts as 1 dc.

Scarf
With largest hook and A, ch 18.
Row 1 Sc in 2nd ch from hook and in each ch across. Ch 1, turn—17 sc.
Row 2 Scblo in each sc across. Ch 1, turn.
Rep Row 2 for pattern until scarf measures 60"/150cm or desired length. End off.

Large Pocket (make 2)
With smallest hook and B, ch 17.
Row 1 Dc in 4th ch from hook and in each ch across. Ch 3, turn—15 dc.
Row 2 Dc in each dc across. Ch 3, turn.
Rep Row 2 for pattern until 11 rows are complete. Ch 1 after final row, do not turn.

Edging
Work 1 rnd rev sc (from left to right) around pocket. Join rnd with sl st in 1st st. End off.

Small Pocket (make 2)
With largest hook and A, ch 13.
Rep instructions for Scarf until work measures 6"/15cm from start—12 sc.

Edging
Work 1 rnd sc around pocket. Join rnd with sl st in 1st st. End off.

Finishing
Scarf Edging
With middle hook and A, work 1 rnd sc around scarf, placing 3 sc in each corner. Join rnd with sl st in 1st sc. End off.

Center Small Pockets on top of Large Pockets and pin into place. Sew together with tapestry needle and A, leaving the top edge open. Center assembled Pockets on scarf, and pin into place. Sew together with tapestry needle and B, leaving the top edge open.
Weave in all ends. ■

hooded scarf

Yarn ④

Lion Brand® *Amazing*, 1¾oz/50g skeins, each approx 147yd/135m (wool/acrylic)
• 6 skeins in Rainforest #825-202

Hooks
• Size L/11 (8.00mm) crochet hook *or size needed to obtain gauge*

Notions
• Tapestry needle
• Straight or safety pins

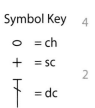

Finished Measurements
Length 43"/110cm from top to bottom of edge after assembly
Width 8"/20cm excluding hood

Gauge
8 sts/1 pattern repeat to 2½"/6.5cm and 6 rows to 4"/10cm over pattern stitch.
Take time to check gauge.

Note
Ch-3 counts as 1 dc throughout.

Stitch Glossary
Shell (3 dc, ch 1, 3 dc) in specified stitch.

Scarf Side (make 2)
Ch 26.
Row 1 Sc in 2nd ch from hook, *sk 3 ch, shell in next ch, sk 3 ch, sc in next ch. Rep from * to end. Ch 3, turn—3 shells + 4 sc.
Row 2 3 dc in 1st sc, sc in next ch-1 sp, *shell in next sc, sc in next ch-1 sp, rep from * across, 4 dc in last sc. Ch 1, turn—2 shells + 3 sc + 2 4-dc shells.
Row 3 Sc in 1st dc, shell in next sc, *sc in next ch-1 sp, shell in next sc. Rep from* across, sc in last dc. Ch 3, turn.
Rep Rows 2–3 for pattern until work measures 28"/71cm from beg, ending with a Row 2.

Hood Shaping Increases
Row 1 Sc in 1st dc, shell in next sc, *sc in next ch-1 sp, shell in next sc. Rep from * across, sc in last dc. Ch 5, turn.
Row 2 Sc in 2nd ch from hook, (2 dc, ch 1, 3 dc) in next sc, *sc in next ch-1 sp, shell in next sc. Rep from * across, 4 dc in last sc. Ch 1, turn—3 shells + 4 sc + 1 4-dc shell.

Row 3 Sc in 1st dc, *shell in next sc, sc in next ch-1 sp. Rep from * across , 4 dc in last sc. Ch 1, turn—3 shells plus 1 4-dc shell.
Row 4 Rep Row 3 of Scarf.
Row 5 Sc in 1st dc, *shell in next sc, sc in next ch-1 sp, rep from * across to last sc, shell in last sc. Ch 4, turn—4 shells + 4 sc.
Row 6 3 dc in 4th ch from hook, sc in next ch-1 sp, *shell in next sc, sc in next ch-1 sp. Rep from * across, 4 dc in last sc. Ch1, turn—3 shells + 4 sc + 2 4-dc shells.
Rows 7–12 Rep Rows 1–6.
Rows 13–15 Rep Row 3 of Scarf, then Rows 2–3 of Scarf once more.
Row 16 3 dc in 1st sc, *sc in next ch-1 sp, shell in next sc. Rep from * 4 times, sc in next ch-1 sp. Leave remaining sts unworked. Ch 1, turn.
Row 17 Sl st in 1st sc and in each of 1st 3 dc, sl st in ch-1 sp, ch 1, *sc in ch-1 sp, shell in next sc. Rep from * across, sc in last dc. End off, leaving a long tail for sewing.

Pocket (make 2)
Ch 23.
Row 1 Dc in 4th ch from hook and in each ch to end. Ch 3, turn—20 dc.
Row 2 Dc in each dc. Ch 3, turn.
Rows 3–11 Repeat Row 2. End off after Row 11.

Pocket Flap (make 2)
Ch 26.
Rep Rows 1–4 of Scarf. End off.

Assembly
Seam scarf sides together starting at center front and up and over the hood until center back seam measures 12"/30cm.
Align pockets with scarf edges and pin in place. Beginning at center back seam, work 1 rnd sc evenly spaced around entire scarf, working through both layers of fabric at each pocket and placing 3 sc in each corner. Join rnd with sl st in 1st sc, end off.
Work 1 row sc evenly spaced along each pocket flap side.
Sew pocket flaps above each pocket.
Weave in all ends. ■

Symbol Key
○ = ch
+ = sc
┬ = dc

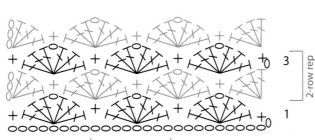

patt rep

2-row rep

sheep scarf

Finished Measurements
44"/112cm by 12"/30.5cm

Gauge
6.5 sts and 4.5 rows to 4"/10cm over dc.
Take time to check gauge.

Notes
Ch-2 does not count as 1 st.
Ch-3 counts as 1 dc.

Hoof Pocket (make 2)
With B and smaller hook ch 12.
Rnd 1 4 dc in 4th ch from hook, dc in each of next 7 ch, 5 dc in next ch, working in opposite side of foundation ch, dc in each of next 7 ch. Join rnd with sl st in top of beg-ch. Ch 3, turn—24 dc.
Rnd 2 Dcblo in each dc around. Join rnd with sl st in top of beg-ch. Ch 3, turn.
Rnd 3 Dc in each dc around. Join rnd with sl st in top of beg-ch. Ch 3, turn.
Rep Rnd 3 for pattern until work measures 8"/20cm tall, not including Rnd 1, which acts as the flat base of the pocket. On final rnd, place stitch marker in st after rnd join just made. End off.

Scarf
Left Side
Row 1 Working along back of folded pocket, with RS facing, larger hook, and A, sc in marked dc and in each of next 10 dc. Remove marker. Ch 1, turn—11 sc.
Row 2 (WS) Sc in 1st sc, *tr in next sc, sc in next sc. Rep from * across. Ch 1, turn.
Row 3 (RS) Sc in each sc and tr across. Ch 1, turn—11 sc.
Row 4 Tr in 1st sc, *sc in next sc, tr in next sc. Rep from * across, sl st in last sc (same st as last tr). Ch 2, turn. Ch-2 does not count as 1 st.
Row 5 Rep Row 3.
Rep Rows 2–5 7 times more or to desired length, ending with a Row 5.

Hood Shaping
Row 1 Sc in 1st sc, (tr in next sc, sc in next sc) 4 times, sl st in next sc, leave remaining st unworked. Ch 1, turn—5 sc + 4 tr.
Row 2 Sc in each sc and tr across 9 sc. End off, leaving a long tail for sewing seam.

Right Side
Rep all instructions up to Hood Shaping.

Hood Shaping
Row 1 Sl st in each of 1st 2 sc, sc in next sc, [tr in next sc, sc in next sc] 4 times—5 sc + 4 tr. End off.

Ears (make 2)
With larger hook and A, ch 6.
Row 1 Sc in 2nd ch from hook and in each ch across. Ch 1, turn—5 sc.
Rows 2–4 Sc in each sc across. Ch 1, turn; end off after Row 4.

Ear Linings (make 2)
With smaller hook and C, ch 8.
Row 1 Dc in 4th ch from hook and in each ch across. Ch 3, turn—7 dc.
Rows 2 and 3 Dc in each dc across. Ch 3, turn after Row 2, end off after Row 3.

Finishing
With WS together, seam Left Side to Right Side beginning at the center front seam and continuing up and over the hood until center back seam measures 11.5"/29cm.
With A work 1 row sc from pocket to pocket along center front opening.
With A work 1 row sc from pocket to pocket along center back opening.
With A, stitch ear lining into each ear.
With A, stitch each ear to hood as shown in photo.
Weave in all ends. ◼

Yarn ④ ⑥
Lion Brand® *Quick and Cozy*, 3½oz/100g skeins, each approx 55yd/50m (nylon)
• 7 skeins in Marshmallow #926-100 (A)
Lion Brand® WOOL-EASE® THICK & QUICK®, 6oz/170g skeins, each approx 106 yd/97 m (acrylic/wool)
• 1 skein Charcoal #640-149 (B)
• 1 skein Blossom #640-103 (C)

Hooks
• Size N/15 (10.00mm) crohet hook
• Size Q/19 (15.00mm) crochet hooks
or size needed to obtain gauge

Notions
• Tapestry needle with a large eye
• Stitch marker

dog walker scarf

Yarn 4

Bernat® *Sheep(ish)* by Vickie Howell, 3oz/85g skeins, each approx 167yd/153m (acrylic/wool)
- 3 skeins in Hot Pink(ish) #0007 (A)
- 2 skeins in Chartreuse(ish) #0020 (B)

Hook
- Size H/8 (5.00mm) crochet hook *or size needed to obtain gauge*

Notions
- Embroidary needle with sharp point
- Straight or safety pins
- ¼yd/¼m zebra print fleece fabric cut into 11 3½"/9 cm squares

Finished Measurements

64"/163cm by 8"/20cm (excluding edging)

Gauge

13 sts and 7 rows to 4"/10cm over dc.
Take time to check gauge.

Note

Ch-3 counts as 1 dc.

Stitch Glossary

Rev sc reverse sc, worked from left to right.

Square Set-up

With sharp embroidary needle, blanket stitch around 5 fleece squares with A and 6 fleece squares with B, making sure there are 8 loops on each side and one on each corner. When turning the corner, place the last st on one side and the 1st st in the next side in the same place on the fabric for a neat, mitered edge.

Large Squares (make 3 A and 4 B)

Rnd 1 Join yarn matching blanket stitch with sl st in any corner st, ch 3, (dc, ch 2, 2 dc) in same corner st, *dc in each blanket st across, (2 dc, ch 2, 2 dc) in corner st; rep from * twice more, dc in each blanket st to end. Join rnd with sl st in top of beg-ch.
Rnd 2 Sl st in next dc, sl st in ch-2 space, ch 3 (dc, ch 3, 2 dc) in same corner, *dc in each dc across, (2 dc, ch 3, 2 dc) in corner; rep from * twice more, dc in each dc to end. Join rnd with sl st in top of beg ch.
Rnd 3 Rep Rnd 2.
Rnd 4 With opposite color, rep Rnd 2. End off.

Small Pocket (make 2)

Rnd 1 With B and matching fleece square, rep Rnd 1 of Large Squares.
Rnd 2 Ch 1, rev sc in each dc and ch-2 sp around. Join rnd with sl st in 1st rev sc. End off.

Large Pocket (make 2)

Rnds 1 and 2 With A and matching fleece square, rep Rnds 1–2 of Large Squares.
Rnd 3 Ch 1, rev sc in each dc and ch-2 sp around. Join rnd with sl st in 1st rev sc. End off.

Finishing

Join Large Squares

Arrange Large Squares so center colors alternate: B, A, B, A, B, A, B.
With RS together of 1 A and 1 B square, join A on wrong side with sl st in corner, ch 1, sc in same corner and each st across to next corner, working only in front loop of st closest to you and back loop of st farthest away. End off.
Rep for remaining 5 squares.
Pin large pockets to end squares matching fleece squares. Sew in place with A.
Pin small pockets to second squares up from end, matching fleece squares. Sew in place with B.

Edging

Rnd 1 Join A with sl st in any st on outer edge of assembled scarf, ch 1, sc in same st, sc around entire scarf placing 3 sc in each corner. Join rnd with sl st in 1st sc. Ch 1, do not turn.
Rnd 1 Rev sc in each sc around, Join rnd with sl st in 1st rev sc. End off.
Weave in all ends. ■

MP3 scarf

Yarn ④
RED HEART *Kids*, 4oz/113g skeins, each approx. 232yd/212m (acrylic)
• 2 skeins in Bikini #2945

Hook
• H/8 (5.0 mm) crochet hook or size needed to obtain gauge

Notions
• Tapestry needle
• Straight or safety pins

▰▰▱▱▱

Finished Measurements
100"/2.5cm by 4"/10cm including edging

Gauge
12 sts and 6 rows to 4"/10cm over pattern st.
Take time to check gauge.

Stitch Glossary
Picot Ch 3, sl st in 3rd ch from hook.
Shell 3 dc in designated st

Note
Ch-3 counts as 1 dc throughout.

Scarf
Ch 13.
Row 1 3 dc in 5th ch from hook, [sk 2 ch, shell in next dc] twice, sk 1 ch, dc in last ch. Ch 3, turn—3 shells + 2 dc.
Row 2 2 dc between 1st and 2nd dc from hook,(shell between 3rd and 4th dc from hook) twice, 2 dc between 3rd and 4th dc from hook, dc in top of t-ch. Ch 3, turn—4 shells.
Row 3 (Shell between 3rd and 4th ch from hook) 3 times, sk 2 dc, dc in last dc. Ch 3, turn. Rep Rows 2–3 for pattern until work measures 100"/254cm from start, ending with a Row 2. End off.

Pockets (make 2)
Rep instructions for Scarf until pocket is 6"/15.5cm long, ending with a Row 3. Ch 1, turn after final row.

Picot Edging
Top Edge
Row 1 Sc in each of 1st 3 dc, picot, (sc in each of next 3 dc, picot) twice, sc in each of last 3 dc. End off.

Bottom Edge
Row 1 Join yarn with sl st in base of dc, ch 1, sc in same dc, sc in next ch, picot, (sc in base of shell and each of next 2 ch, picot) 3 times, sc in base of last dc. End off.

Finishing
Pin edged pockets onto scarf so that bottom of pockets are 16"/40.5cm up from short each end of scarf.

Edging
Join yarn with sl st anywhere along edge of scarf.
Rnd 1 Ch 1, sc in same st as sl st, sc evenly spaced around entire scarf, working a picot after every 3rd sc, placing 3 sc in each corner, and joining the pockets to the scarf by working through both layers when you come to them. Join rnd with sl st in 1st sc. End off.
Weave in all ends. ▪

easy one-stitch scarf

Yarn **(4)**
RED HEART *Boutique Unforgettable*, 3½oz/100g skeins, each approx 279yd/256m (acrylic)
• 4 skeins in Dragonfly #3935

Hook
• Size G/6 (4.00 mm) crochet hook *or size needed to obtain gauge*

Notions
• Tapestry needle
• Straight or safety pins

Finished Measurements
8"/20cm by 80"/203cm including edging

Gauge
15 sts and 8 rows to 4"/10cm over double crochet.
Take time to check gauge.

Note
Ch-3 counts as 1 dc.

Scarf
Ch 28.
Row 1 Dc in 4th ch from hook and in each ch across. Ch 3, turn—26 dc.
Row 2 Dc in each dc across. Ch 3, turn.
Rep Row 2 for pattern until work measures 98"/249cm from start. End off.

Assembly
Fold each short edge up 9"/23cm to form pocket, and pin into place.

Edging
Work on both long sides.
Join yarn at fold of one pocket with a sl st through both layers, ch 3.
Row 1 Work 1 row dc evenly spaced across long edge of scarf, working through both layers of fabric at each pocket. End off.
Weave in all ends. ■

my notes